The San Francisco Earthquake of 1906

by Marc Tyler Nobleman

Content Adviser: Peggy Hellweg,
Berkeley Seismological Laboratory,
University of California, Berkeley

Reading Adviser: Rosemary G. Palmer, Ph.D.,
Department of Literacy, College of Education,
Boise State University

Compass Point Books ✦ Minneapolis, Minnesota

Compass Point Books
3109 West 50th Street, #115
Minneapolis, MN 55410

Visit Compass Point Books on the Internet at *www.compasspointbooks.com*
or e-mail your request to *custserv@compasspointbooks.com*

On the cover: Houses on Howard Street after the San Francisco earthquake of April 18, 1906

Photographs ©: The Granger Collection, New York, cover, 15, 23, 24; Prints Old & Rare, back cover (far left); Library of Congress, back cover, 9, 18, 19, 25; Mary Evans Picture Library, 4; San Francisco History Center, San Francisco Public Library, 5, 14; North Wind Picture Archives, 7, 8, 32; Science VU/GSFC/Visuals Unlimited, 11; Corbis, 12, 17, 21, 33, 34; Historic Photo Archive/Getty Images, 13; The Illustrated London News Picture Library, London, UK/The Bridgeman Art Library, 20; Courtesy of Army Art Collection, U.S. Army Center of Military History, 27; Collections Branch, U.S. Army Center of Military History, 28; Denver Public Library, Western History Collection, Joseph Collier, C-304, 30; Pictorial Parade/Getty Images, 31; Justin Sullivan/Getty Images, 37; Hulton Archive/Getty Images, 38; Digital Vision, 40.

Editor: Anthony Wacholtz
Page Production: Bobbie Nuytten
Photo Researcher: Eric Gohl
Cartographer: XNR Productions, Inc.
Library Consultant: Kathleen Baxter

Creative Director: Keith Griffin
Editorial Director: Carol Jones
Managing Editor: Catherine Neitge

Library of Congress Cataloging-in-Publication Data
Nobleman, Marc Tyler.
  The San Francisco earthquake of 1906 / by Marc Tyler Nobleman.
     p. cm.—(We the people)
  Includes bibliographical references and index.
  Audience: Grades 4-6.
  ISBN-13: 978-0-7565-2460-9 (library binding)
  ISBN-10: 0-7565-2460-1 (library binding)
  ISBN-13: 978-0-7565-3221-5 (paperback)
  ISBN-10: 0-7565-3221-3 (paperback)
1. San Francisco Earthquake, Calif., 1906—Juvenile literature. 2. Earthquakes—California—San Francisco—History—20th century—Juvenile literature. 3. Fires—California—San Francisco—History—20th century—Juvenile literature. 4. San Francisco (Calif.)—History—20th century—Juvenile literature. I. Title. II. Series.
  F869.S357N63 2007
  979.4'61051—dc22   2006027090

TABLE OF CONTENTS

Less Than a Minute 4

The Instant City 8

The Man Who Could Have Saved

San Francisco 14

No Need of Bells 17

Go or Stay 20

The Army Steps In 24

"There Is No Water" 29

Fighting Fire with Fire 33

The Golden Hydrant 36

Glossary 42

Did You Know? 43

Important Dates 44

Important People 45

Want to Know More? 46

Index 48

LESS THAN A MINUTE

Twenty-two minutes before sunrise on Wednesday, April 18, 1906, 12-year-old Elsie Cross was shaken awake.

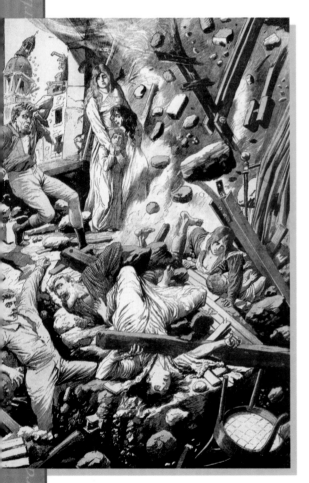

Members of a family were horror-stricken as their house collapsed on top of them.

Like everyone else who lived in San Francisco, California, Elsie was used to minor earthquakes every now and then that were "gentle and mild."

But the shaking did not stop, and it did not stay gentle. In seconds, it felt as if the room—the entire house—was being jerked up and down and from side to side all at once. Elsie had heard that the safest place to stand during an earthquake was under a doorway. She scrambled to the one in her bedroom and said a

4

prayer. The furniture, as Elsie later described it, "danced a jig." Household items were tossed about. Drawers flew out of bureaus, scattering their contents haphazardly. A music box was hurled to the floor, where it played a cheerful song amid a scene that was anything but cheerful. However, the absurdity of it did manage to make Elsie laugh.

Bolting from her doorway, she saw her family in

Four women posed under a mangled building after the earthquake.

other rooms. As her father tried to reach her mother and brother, he was thrown across the floor—twice. The chimney broke through the roof and plummeted to the basement. Elsie did not know it yet, but the same thing was happening to many other chimneys in many other houses across the city at the same time.

Between 45 and 60 seconds after the earthquake started, San Francisco was quiet again.

Everyone blinked. Mr. Cross told his family to get dressed quickly, adding that they should run to the street immediately if another tremor hit. Minutes later, the family went outside and was shocked by what they saw. The house across the street had shifted over 9 feet (2.75 meters). The house next to that had sunk 10 feet (3 m) into the soft soil. The San Francisco that Elsie had known had been shaken into shambles in less than a minute.

Surveying the damage, Cross supposed the quake was over, but he had a foreboding thought. He knew that countless homes had candles, stoves, and heaters that would have

A street was blocked with debris and collapsed buildings after the earthquake.

been lit when the ground shook. The main trouble would be fire.

Elsie's father was tragically right. Much of San Francisco—one of the largest American cities with one of the most modern fire departments in the world—was about to burn out of existence.

THE INSTANT CITY

In 1848, a group of laborers discovered gold in sparsely populated northern California. Hoping to claim their own share of the riches, thousands of people rushed to the region. Population figures vary widely, but by many accounts, San Francisco ballooned from fewer than 1,000

Thousands of prospectors traveled to California to search for gold during the Gold Rush.

inhabitants in 1848 to at least 25,000 by the end of the following year, instantly turning it into a city. Its rapid growth continued for the rest of the 19th century.

By 1906, approximately 400,000 people—including 30,000 immigrants—called San Francisco home. It had become the leading port on the West Coast of the United States. Its Wild West roots still showed, with 1,000 saloons and the highest murder rate in the country for a city its size. Yet San Francisco was also a commercial and cultural center. The city had a crowded business district, two opera houses, five daily newspapers, nine libraries, and several luxurious hotels.

By 1850, San Francisco had grown into a bustling city.

The scenery was attractive, too. San Francisco sat on a peninsula along one of the world's largest natural harbors. Residents could enjoy breezes and lovely views of the water from many of the city's 42 hills.

Underneath those seemingly peaceful hills, however, was—and is—a geologic time bomb: the San Andreas Fault. The surface of Earth is made of large plates of rock called tectonic plates. Pressure from underground heat causes the plates to move. At times, people feel that movement as an earthquake. The San Andreas Fault is a place where two of these plates meet. It stretches 800 miles (1,280 kilometers) along the coast of California, between San Francisco and San Diego.

At 5:12 A.M. on April 18, 1906, with a loud rumbling, the sides of the northern 300 miles (480 km) of the San Andreas Fault moved alongside each other in opposite directions. This occurred with a force so powerful that only a few places in recorded history had experienced something similar. Usually, the plates slid 2 inches (5 cm) a year. That

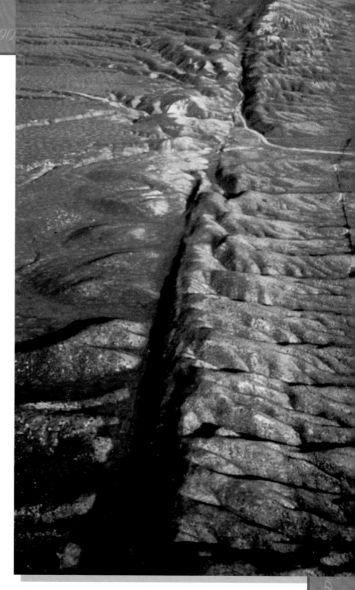

The San Andreas Fault

moment, the plates slid 15 feet (4.6 m) past each other, stretching until they snapped like an enormous rubber band.

In doing so, they thrust everything above them into sudden and massive chaos. A street preacher shouted, "Haven't I warned you?" In Chinatown, people screamed, "The earth dragon has awakened!" One man yelled, "The city must be saved!"

Some of the cracks left in the surface by the earthquake were 28 feet (8.54 m) wide. Earthquake waves raced out from the epicenter, or starting point of the earthquake, at 8,000 miles (12,800 km) an hour. Today, scientists are uncer-

*The earthquake caused sections of the ground to split,
creating a long crack down the middle of a street.*

tain about the location of the epicenter, but many think it was in the Pacific Ocean, about 2 miles (3.2 km) off the west coast of San Francisco. People as far away as Los Angeles and central Nevada felt the shaking, but San Francisco received the full effect of the earthquake.

The scale we use today to measure the energy released by earthquakes—the moment magnitude scale—had not been invented in 1906. If it had, scientists estimate that the San Francisco quake would have registered a magnitude of 7.8. That is classified as "major."

The aftermath was unthinkable. Everything from streetlights and chimneys to towering buildings toppled, sometimes crushing people to death. In areas where the ground was soft, wet soil instead of solid rock, some buildings sank as if they were in quicksand. One police officer saw a street rippling toward him like an ocean wave. Streetcar tracks bent in half, and water mains ruptured throughout the city.

The "instant city" had been split apart in an instant.

Rubble and toppled buildings covered the city after the earthquake.

THE MAN WHO COULD HAVE SAVED SAN FRANCISCO

One of the first deaths from the earthquake would have an effect on the city's response to the disaster. The earthquake had dislodged the giant dome from the California Theater and Hotel near the fire station. Dennis Sullivan, the

respected chief of the San Francisco Fire Department, and his wife were sleeping in the fire station when the dome crashed through the roof. He acted quickly, covering his wife with a mattress, but he was seriously injured. His wife survived, but he died soon after.

14 *Dennis Sullivan (1854–1906)*

For years, Sullivan had told city officials that San Francisco did not seem prepared for a severe earthquake or fire. The city had endured numerous earthquakes, particularly in 1836, 1865, 1868, and 1892. Between 1849 and 1851, at least six large fires had ravaged the city. Considering the town's history of earthquakes and fires, everyone knew there would be more.

The San Francisco earthquake of 1865 split a wooden building in two.

15

Earthquakes are generally unpredictable and always unstoppable. Fires, on the other hand, can be prevented or extinguished. In most cases, the key to fighting fires is water, but the city's water system was insufficient. Buildings were not yet required to have sprinkler systems. Of the 63 cisterns throughout the city, more than half needed repair. Some were even filled with trash instead of water.

Sullivan had urged city officials to fix these problems, but they did not listen. Perhaps they did not believe there was a real threat, or perhaps certain corrupt politicians refused to take action unless they could profit from it themselves.

Even though Sullivan's suggestions were ignored, it is likely that more of the city would have been protected if he had lived. Sullivan's next-in-command was Chief John Dougherty, and Chief Patrick Shaughnessy was just below him. They had their strengths, but they did not have Sullivan's lifesaving instincts.

But now, he was gone.

NO NEED OF BELLS

The San Francisco Fire Department consisted of 568 firefighters and 48 firehouses. Hundreds of horses and dogs assisted them. The horses pulled hook and ladder wagons—the 1906 versions of fire trucks. The dogs ran ahead of the

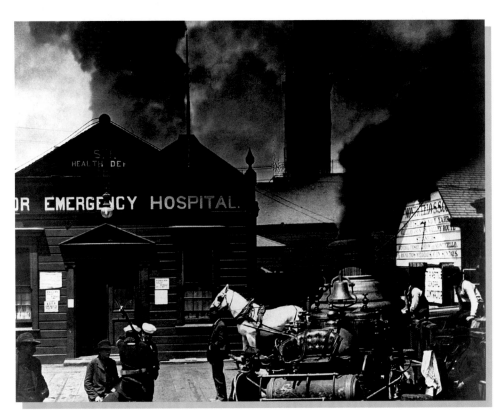

Firefighters tried to protect San Francisco's Harbor Emergency Hospital.

17

Water from a hook and ladder wagon soaked a block of ignited buildings.

fire trucks, barking to signal people to get out of the way.

Although the city's water supply was inadequate, its fire department was up-to-date. Most of its steamers were less than eight years old, and all were inspected frequently. The city was equipped with an efficient alarm system, including 424 street alarm boxes, bells in most firefighters' homes, and even 30 bells in businesses that were popular with firefighters. However, there was no need of bells that day. Firefighters could see flames everywhere, without even leaving their firehouses.

At 8:14 A.M., the first of many noticeable aftershocks rattled San Francisco, causing more panic. Most telephone and telegraph lines were knocked out. The fire department dispatch system went dead.

San Francisco was cut off from the rest of the world, and firefighters across the city could not communicate with one another.

The smoke and flames could be seen from everywhere in the city.

GO OR STAY

In 1906, buildings in San Francisco were lit by gas lamps—and 90 percent of the buildings were made of wood. These flammable structures were often packed tightly together, which allowed fire to spread more easily. In the first 30 minutes after the earthquake, the fire department had received word of 52 blazes across the city.

Fifteen minutes after the fire began, a San Francisco building was destroyed.

Around 10 A.M., a woman was cooking breakfast but did not know that her chimney had been damaged. As a result, sparks escaped and set her house on fire. This became known as the "ham and eggs" fire. It hopped from one building to another throughout the city, consuming many structures, including City Hall. It had taken 20 years to build—and about two minutes to collapse. The fire also

City Hall could not withstand the earthquake's destructive power.

took the Mechanics Pavilion, the largest auditorium in the city, which had been converted to a temporary hospital earlier that morning. The ham and eggs fire would scorch more property than any of the other fires.

Thousands of people, both poor and rich, hurried along the rubble-strewn streets. Many headed for the ferry to take them across the bay to Oakland and other cities. Others left by train, free of charge, courtesy of the railroad companies. Still more fled on foot, shoving or dragging trunks stuffed with their most valuable belongings. Some people wore several layers of clothes rather than carry them. Many would never see their homes again.

Some people stayed put, either confident that the fire would not reach them or determined to try to protect their homes if it did. The military, which had been dispatched to the city to keep order, forced many people to evacuate, sometimes at gunpoint. That tactic was later criticized because those homeowners were clearly helping the firefighters by trying to save property on their own. Other

San Francisco residents watched from a hillside as the flames engulfed their city.

people left their homes but stayed in the city. They camped out in vacant lots, parks, and graveyards, where nothing could burn or fall on them.

THE ARMY STEPS IN

When the earthquake struck, General Frederick Funston was in charge of the military base in San Francisco. He had served bravely in several wars, but he had never handled a peacetime crisis. At 6:30 A.M., he had ordered 1,700 troops to report for duty. Historians feel that Funston made an error in judgment by calling in armed soldiers during a peacetime emergency.

Frederick Funston (1865–1917)

San Francisco Mayor Eugene Schmitz heard that people were looting in the burning city. He instructed the army

to shoot anyone caught doing anything criminal. Residents
thought that meant Schmitz had declared martial law in
San Francisco, but legally, he did not have the authority to

Armed soldiers were stationed throughout San Francisco after the earthquake.

do that. By midday, 5,000 flyers stating the mayor's shoot-to-kill proclamation had been handed out or posted on streetlights and doors. Funston questioned the decision, but Schmitz said he would take responsibility for it. The proclamation did not help the military to keep order. Instead, it caused greater havoc.

Some of the soldiers followed the shoot-to-kill order. Like most people in the city, the soldiers may have been confused or scared, and they were sometimes careless. At times, a soldier shot a person without first asking what he or she was doing. Some people had no choice but to take things for their loved ones—such as milk for babies—from abandoned shops. Sometimes people were looting items that were about to be burned anyway, not for personal gain, but for basic survival. Regardless, the soldiers only saw illegal acts and carried out their orders. Though it was once believed that the army killed 500 people during the fire, newer research indicates that the actual figure is probably much lower.

Soldiers forced a civilian to use his wagon to deliver supplies into the burning city.

Hundreds of refugee tents were constructed for victims of the earthquake and fires.

The army had a positive effect, too. It provided food, drinking water, and refugee camps. A small group of naval officers under the direction of Lieutenant Frederick Newton Freeman boldly protected the docks from the infernos. Their success ensured that more supplies could be shipped into the city and that people could leave by ferry.

"There Is No Water"

Dust from crumbled buildings swirled through the air, and pillars of black smoke twisted up from San Francisco. Although the fire moved slowly, the danger was escalating.

Smaller fires were merging into larger blazes, devouring apartments and majestic historical buildings. Firefighters battled to contain the fires and were able to put some out, but San Francisco simply did not have enough accessible water. Too many water mains had ruptured. Many hydrants were dry. Sometimes the firefighters tried to use hoses to suck up water from the sewers, without luck. In desperation, some extinguished fires by dumping sand on them.

The absence of water not only thwarted the firefighters' attempts to stop the fires, but it also made it harder for them to tolerate the heat. They took off their shirts, dunked them in whatever groundwater they found, and wrapped the damp cloth around their heads. Some firefighters rolled

29

in muddy puddles.

Police officers and civilians also risked their lives to rescue others. Many climbed on piles of fallen buildings to get to victims who were trapped underneath. When people could not be freed as the fire approached, some begged to be shot before they would burn to death. Some people tried to protect their homes or other buildings by wetting the walls using mops and whatever liquid they had.

In 1906, the Call Building was the tallest structure in San Francisco.

30

The Call Building was ravaged by fire, and the earthquake caused the base to sink 2 feet (60 centimeters) below the level of the sidewalk.

At a meeting of town officials on the night of April 18, General Funston announced, "There is no water." As if that news wasn't bad enough, the wind was beginning to pick

31

Soldiers, policemen, and civilians tried to save people from the wreckage.

up. With the wind spreading the fire more quickly and not enough water to put it out, another method of stopping the fire was needed to salvage what was left of the city.

FIGHTING FIRE WITH FIRE

So far, the people of San Francisco had failed to defeat the fire, so they decided to dynamite enough buildings to create a firebreak—a border where there is nothing to burn. Although the firefighters would have rather not used dynamite, they thought it was necessary to prevent the

Smoke billowed from the city as the fire continued to grow.

entire city from burning.

Some buildings had been dynamited that afternoon, but that only created more problems. None of the men setting off the dynamite had done it before. In addition, they were not using real dynamite. The army had mistakenly sent a less-powerful explosive, which no one realized. These explosives blew out windows and sent scraps of wood through the air. Those wood pieces were often aflame, so when

A newspaper's headlines portrayed the hopelessness of the disaster.

they landed, they started a new fire.

On the evening of Thursday, April 19, firefighters prepared to make their last stand on Van Ness Avenue, a wide street where many wealthy San Franciscans lived. The firefighters sprayed water from a remarkable hose line that snaked all the way to the bay, more than a mile away. But the army had also set its sights on Van Ness. On Friday morning, the soldiers dynamited a row of mansions on one side of the street. That time, it worked; the fire ran out of material to burn and went out. Still, more fires continued to burn elsewhere.

THE GOLDEN HYDRANT

Fires raged in the Mission District, in what was the southwestern part of the city, and along the waterfront. In the Mission District, firefighters and 300 civilians teamed up to push the heavy fire engines up hills. The heat was so intense that some of the men ripped doors off houses to use as shields. They attacked the fire with whatever they had. Early Saturday, April 21, they were thrilled to find a hydrant with water—enough to smother the fire in that area. To this day, the historic hydrant is painted gold every year.

At the piers and wharfs, Lieutenant Freeman and his crew continued to work to protect the docks despite extreme exhaustion. Naval reinforcements arrived, and together they showered the flames with water.

Just after 7 A.M. that Saturday, after three days of madness, the people had beaten the fires. The firefighters had worked continuously since the quake, barely eating or

The San Francisco Fire Chief, Joanne Hayes-White, coated the famous fire hydrant with gold spray paint on April 18, 2006.

sleeping. Most did not even know what happened to their own families and homes. That night, a hard rain fell.

Approximately 3,000 people died during the earth-

A woman cooked dinner for two children at the Golden Gate Park relief camp.

quake and fires, including Chief Sullivan, another fire-
fighter, and one police officer. More than 28,000 buildings
and 500 city blocks were lost. Around 225,000 people were
left homeless. Amazingly, the quake itself had caused only

2 percent of the devastation; the fires did the rest.

Aid and supplies poured in from across the country and around the world. James Duval Phelan, who had been mayor of San Francisco from 1897 to 1902, led the relief effort. He was one of the citizens who had pulled people from the ruins only days before.

The people of San Francisco began to rebuild their

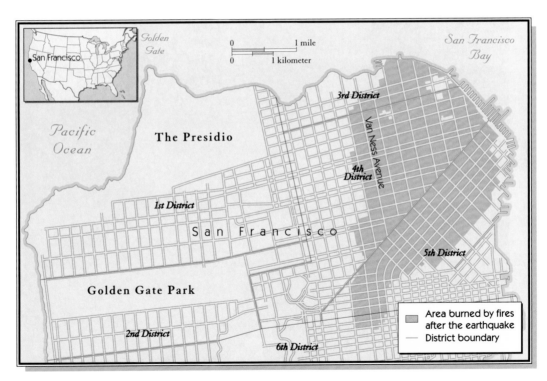

Fires consumed much of the 3rd, 4th, and 5th Districts in San Francisco.

city and their lives even before the fires were out. Yet in their haste, they constructed buildings that were just as vulnerable as the ones that had been destroyed. Eventually, the

Present-day San Francisco

40

city would create new building codes.

The people of San Francisco preferred to remember those four days in April as the Great Fire, not the Great Earthquake. They thought the threat of an earthquake might keep tourists and new businesses away, but the threat of a fire would not since fires can happen in any city. By the fall of 1907, San Francisco showed little evidence of the catastrophe.

A study released by the United States Geological Survey in 2003 said there is a 62 percent chance of another major earthquake striking the San Francisco area in the next 30 years. Although people who live there may know the risk, they love their city enough to stay—and perhaps even fight for it as their ancestors did more than a century ago.

GLOSSARY

aftershocks—smaller earthquakes that occur after the main earthquake

cisterns—underground tanks that store water

epicenter—the point on the surface of Earth directly above the focus of an earthquake

fault—a place where two pieces of Earth's crust have moved past each other

firebreak—an area cleared of flammable material in order to stop fire from spreading

hook and ladder wagon—a simple fire engine

looting—taking advantage of a chaotic situation by stealing

magnitude—the measure of how big or strong something is

peninsula—a piece of land that sticks out into a body of water

refugee—a person who flees from home for safety

saloons—bars

DID YOU KNOW?

- Not far from where Elsie Cross lived, a 4-year-old boy was playing in his family's garden when an aftershock caused him to fall face-first into a brick wall. The impact broke his nose, which was never straightened. His name was Ansel Adams, and he grew up to be one of the best-known wilderness photographers of the 20th century.

- On the first day of the disaster, the first three floors of the Valencia Hotel were swallowed by the earth, killing dozens in the collapse. Unharmed people on the fourth floor were able to step out directly onto the street.

- Ten employees of the beautiful new U.S. Post Office and Courthouse—which had taken 12 years to build—valiantly defended it from flames. They removed all curtains and pushed furniture and other items to the center of each room. Two rooms burned, but they saved the rest.

- In the days immediately after the disaster, the mayor banned indoor fires. People moved their stoves to the street to cook.

IMPORTANT DATES

Timeline

| 1848 | Gold lures adventurers to what is now San Francisco, and the city's population expands quickly. |

| 1900 | Chief Dennis Sullivan begins filing reports stating that San Francisco needed to improve its water system, but city officials ignore him. |

| 1906 | On April 18, a massive earthquake rocks San Francisco, crumbling the city and starting fires that burn for more than three days. The number of people killed is estimated to be 3,000. |

| 1907 | After an intensive year of rebuilding, there is little trace of the disaster in San Francisco. |

| 1909 | San Francisco adopts a new building code, though thousands of new structures are already built. The code continues to be revised numerous times throughout the 20th century as more is learned about how buildings perform during earthquakes. |

| 2006 | San Francisco observes the 100th anniversary of the earthquake and fires. A handful of survivors speak to the crowds. |

IMPORTANT PEOPLE

FREDERICK NEWTON FREEMAN (1875–?)

Lieutenant in the U.S. Navy who tirelessly fought the fire on the waterfront after the earthquake

FREDERICK FUNSTON (1865–1917)

Army general who led the military response to the earthquake and fires; a brave, dedicated soldier but inexperienced with peacetime crises

JAMES DUVAL PHELAN (1861–1930)

Former mayor of San Francisco who was placed in charge of the Relief Committee after the earthquake; he was elected to the U.S. Senate in 1914 and served one term

EUGENE SCHMITZ (1864–1928)

Mayor of San Francisco who called in armed soldiers at the time of the earthquake; also in 1906, he was convicted of bribery and graft, but the conviction was overturned

DENNIS SULLIVAN (1854–1906)

Chief of the San Francisco Fire Department at the time of the earthquake who died from injuries he received during the disaster

WANT TO KNOW MORE?

At the Library

Chippendale. Lisa A. *The San Francisco Earthquake of 1906*. New York: Chelsea House Publishers, 2001.

Cooke, Tim. *1906 San Francisco Earthquake*. Milwaukee: Gareth Stevens Publishing, 2005.

Tanaka, Shelley. *Earthquake!: On a Peaceful Spring Morning Disaster Strikes San Francisco*. New York: Hyperion Books for Children, 2004.

Worth, Richard. *The San Francisco Earthquake*. New York: Facts on File, 2005.

On the Web

For more information on this topic, use FactHound.

1. Go to *www.facthound.com*

2. Type in this book ID: 0756524601

3. Click on the *Fetch It* button.

FactHound will find the best Web sites for you.

46

On the Road

**San Francisco Fire Department
Museum**
655 Presidio Ave.
San Francisco, CA 94115-2424
415/563-4630
Museum with artifacts from the 1906
San Francisco fire department

**San Francisco Museum and
Historical Society**
P.O. Box 420470
San Francisco, CA 94142-0470
415/775-1111
Museum to open in 2009 in the Old
Mint, one of the few structures to sur-
vive the earthquake and fires in 1906

Look for more We the People books about this era:

The 19th Amendment
The Berlin Airlift
The Civil Rights Act of 1964
The Dust Bowl
Ellis Island
The Great Depression
The Korean War
Navajo Code Talkers

Pearl Harbor
The Persian Gulf War
September 11
The Sinking of the USS Indianapolis
The Statue of Liberty
The Titanic
The Tuskegee Airmen
The Vietnam Veterans Memorial

A complete list of We the People titles is available on our Web site:
www.compasspointbooks.com

INDEX

aftershocks, 19
alarm boxes, 18

building codes, 41

California Theater and Hotel, 14
Chinatown, 11
City Hall, 21
communication, 19
Cross, Elsie, 4–6
Cross, Mr., 6–7

damage, 5, 6, 11, 13, 14, 19, 21–22, 29, 34–35, 38–39
deaths, 13, 14, 26, 30, 37–38
docks, 28, 36
Dougherty, John, 16
drinking water, 28
dynamite, 33–34, 35

epicenter, 11–12
evacuation, 22–23, 28

fire department, 7, 14, 16, 17–19, 20
fire dogs, 17–18
fire engines. *See* hook and ladder wagons.

firebreaks, 33–34, 35
firefighters, 17, 18, 19, 22, 29, 33, 35, 36–37, 38
fires, 15, 16, 20–22, 28, 29, 30, 32, 33, 34–35, 36, 38, 39, 40, 41
Freeman, Frederick Newton, 28, 36
Funston, Frederick, 24, 26, 31

gas lamps, 20
gold rush, 8
Great Fire, 41

"ham and eggs" fire, 21, 22
hook and ladder wagons, 17, 36
hydrants, 29, 36

immigrants, 9

looting, 24–25, 26

magnitude, 12
martial law, 25
Mechanics Pavilion, 22
military, 22, 24–25, 26, 35, 36
Mission District, 36

Phelan, James Duval, 39

police officers, 13, 30, 38
population, 8–9

reconstruction, 39–41
refugees, 22–23, 28
rescues, 30, 39

San Andreas Fault, 10–11
San Francisco Fire Department, 7, 14, 16, 17–19, 20
Schmitz, Eugene, 24–25, 26
Shaughnessy, Patrick, 16
shoot-to-kill order, 24–26
Sullivan, Dennis, 14, 15, 16, 38

tectonic plates, 10–11
telegraph lines, 19
telephone lines, 19
tourism, 41

United States Geological Survey, 41

Van Ness Avenue, 35

water, 10, 13, 16, 18, 28, 29–30, 31, 32, 35, 36
wind, 31–32

About the Author

Marc Tyler Nobleman is the author of more than 50 books for young people. He writes regularly for magazines including *Nickelodeon* and has written for The History Channel. He is also a cartoonist whose single panels have appeared in more than 100 international publications including *The Wall Street Journal*, *Good Housekeeping*, and *Forbes*. He lives with his wife and daughter in Connecticut.